Robert E. Lee
A History Book for Kids

Robert E. Lee's grandkids surely wanted to hear about the war from their grandfather.

Robert, a humble man, probably had to find a way to talk about this tragic American event.

A wise person always finds the "lesser of two evils" to tell this historical story, because young people will continue to investigate the truth.

Robert E. Lee: A History Book for Kids Copyright © 2021 By Anne Wilson Smith

ALL RIGHTS RESERVED. No part of this publication may be reproduced, distributed, or transmitted in any form or by any means, including photocopying, recording, or other electronic or mechanical methods, or by any information storage and retrieval system without the prior written permission of the publisher, except in the case of very brief quotations embodied in critical reviews and certain other noncommercial uses permitted by copyright law.

Produced in the Republic of South Carolina by
SHOTWELL PUBLISHING LLC
Post Office Box 2592
Columbia, So. Carolina 29202
www.ShotwellPublishing.com

Artwork and design by Gregory G. Newson

Acknowledgments: Artist's models; Thomas Lee Jessee as Robert E. Lee and Sara Gonzalez as Mary Anna Custis Lee

ISBN: 978-1-947660-44-1

10 9 8 7 6 5 4 3 2 1

Robert E. Lee
A History Book for Kids

Written and created by
Anne Wilson Smith

Artwork and design by
Gregory G. Newson

Robert Edward Lee
was born January 19, 1807,
at Stratford Mansion in Virginia.

He came from a family of people who helped build the United States of America.

Two of Robert's uncles had signed the Declaration of Independence.

Young Robert was very close to his mother, Anne, who was often ill.

Robert learned to be kind and considerate by caring for her.

Robert worked very hard in school.

He was known for being a smart and well-disciplined student.

After high school, Robert attended West Point

He was appointed by Senator Andrew Jackson, who later became President.

Robert was a model cadet. He was a top student, and never once received a demerit for bad behavior.

Robert married a charming Southern belle from a respected family.

Her name was Mary Custis, and she was the great-granddaughter of Martha Washington, the first First Lady.

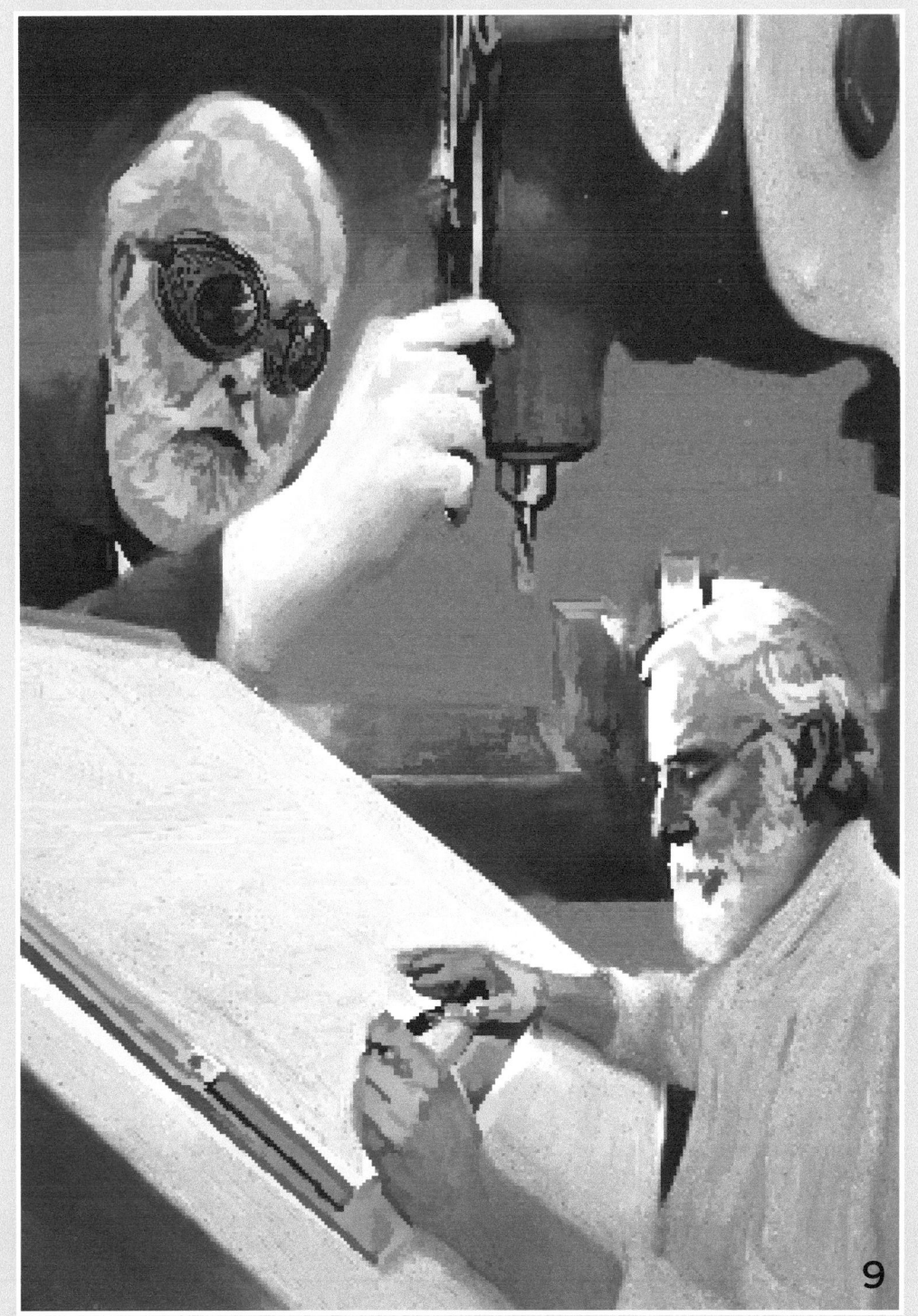

Robert had joined the army as an engineer.

He worked hard to do every task well.

People began to admire him for his excellent character and abilities.

As an army Captain, Robert fought in the Mexican War. It was his first time in battle.

One of his war duties was to go on missions to collect important information. It was sometimes dangerous, but Captain Lee was always determined.

One dark night, Captain Lee had to cross a dangerous field of sharp volcanic rock during a rain storm. Many men could not even cross it during the day!

When he succeeded in this nearly impossible task, the Army Generals praised his courage and skill. He was now known as a real soldier!

Robert then went out West to help the United States conquer the new frontier.

Sometimes he met with Native Americans.

Next, Robert served as superintendent of the Military Academy at West Point where he had once been a student.

When Mary's father died, Robert returned to their home in Virginia to help the family.

There was much work to be done.

Mary's father had passed down slaves.

Robert was to free them in five years, and he did. He helped them find paid work.

Robert thought slavery should be ended, but it would be best to do it gradually over time so the slaves could learn to be independent.

Meanwhile, trouble was brewing between the Northern and Southern states. Some Southern states thought the North was being unfair to them. The South was paying most of the taxes, but the North was making most of the important decisions.

Some people thought the conflict might lead to war.

Robert hoped the states could work out their problems peacefully and the Union would last.

The Southern States' people voted to leave the Union.

South Carolina had been the first state to vote to leave the Union. President Lincoln sent an Army and Navy expedition to occupy Fort Sumter in the middle of Charleston Harbour.

The Confederates bombarded and took over Fort Sumter. Lincoln declared war on the Southern States.

The Confederates fired a shot to warn the Union Navy to go away.

The Yankees fired back.

War had begun.

Robert's home state, Virginia, had not yet decided what to do.

Finally a vote was held. Virginia would join the Confederate states in seceding from the Union.

The United States leaders knew Robert was the best soldier in the Army. They asked him to lead US forces in the War.

Robert faced a terrible decision.

He had spent his life as a proud soldier in the US Army. Now the Army would be fighting against the home he loved, his country, Virginia.

What would he do?

Robert thought very hard.
He prayed to God.

He remembered his father, Henry, said he should always defend Virginia, no matter what he had to sacrifice.

Robert knew what he must do.

He could not fight against the home and people he loved.

Robert resigned from the US Army.

Soon after, Robert accepted a position as a General in the the Confederate Army.

He knew that the US Army was very powerful, and that fighting them would be very difficult.

Lee's army was always short of food. On one occasion a farmer donated a flock of chickens. One bird stood out from all the others.

After a few days, the chicken was given a name: Nellie. The General loved his poached eggs, so Nellie was granted amnesty by the general himself.

Southerners had fewer soldiers and fewer supplies than Yankees.

Sometimes soldiers were very cold, and had no shoes to wear.

Some of the soldiers were very old or very young.

But Robert was a brilliant general, and the Southern soldiers were very brave and determined.

Many people were amazed that the band of ragamuffins could fight so well against such a powerful enemy.

They fought the Union Army for four years.

Even though they fought their hardest, the Union Army was too big and strong. Many, many Confederate soldiers died.

General Lee did not want to surrender, but he now knew the South could not win, and that it would only hurt his people more if they kept fighting.

General Lee met with General Grant to surrender. He wore his finest uniform.

After the war, Robert returned home to his people in Virginia. They loved him for what he had done for them.

Lee's gray horse Traveler, which he rode throughout the war, was almost as famous as Lee himself. Traveler was as calm and steady under fire as his rider. After the war was over, Traveler retired with Lee to Lexington and was his constant companion.

Though defeated, Lee was famous all over the world. He turned down many business offers that would have made him rich to share the fate of his people.

Back in Virginia, Robert helped build up struggling Washington College, which was later renamed Washington & Lee University.

He wanted to make it a place for young Southerners to learn and to become good citizens.

Robert enjoyed a peaceful life with his family for five years, until he became ill and died.

Southerners today can be proud to claim the smart, brave, and honorable Robert Edward Lee as one of our own.

www.ingramcontent.com/pod-product-compliance
Lightning Source LLC
Chambersburg PA
CBHW042110090526

44592CB00004B/70